SHADOW LIGHT

Warren Baker

Fomite
Burlington, VT

ISBN-13: 978-1-959984-76-4
Library of Congress Control Number: 2025933599

Fomite
58 Peru Street
Burlington, VT 05401
www.fomitepress.com

6/7/2025

For Sharon … always

Shadow Light

Walk woods and fields at dusk.
Watch shadows emerge

on the east side of a hillock,
in the basin of a hollow

or a tiny cavern under the edge
of a boulder. See how shape

and texture form, fleeting, like catching
sight of a wren's wing tip as it flits past.

Shadow light holds for seconds only.
Step inside while you can.

Contents

3. Taking Your Turn

4. Harvest

5. Lay of the Land

Keep looking for the mystery in the commonplace.
John Clarke

1. Mettle and Pluck

Follow the grain in your own wood.
Rev. Howard Thurman

Breathing the Cedars

For years I've meant to clear the tangle
of brush and vines from three cedar trunks
and their branches, but other chores came first.

For this hour then, nothing matters more
than edging with clippers and hand saw
from one gnarled root cluster to the next,

cutting at ground level, patting back in place
sheaths of moss I scuff with my boots.
I step back to look. Now unfettered,

the cedars welcome me like old friends
who long ago forgave the slights I delivered
when preoccupied and have regretted ever since.

Encumbered

Wild turkey tracks mark a path up the hill,
leaf cover cleared where they stopped to scratch.
Around rocks, along a downed white birch,
I follow the trail to the top where I sit and wait
for the sounds of the woods to return.
A thrush appears, balanced on a barberry bush.
Crickets resume their thrum. Beside me, a box turtle
stirs from its camouflage to begin its slog down
to the creek. I come here often, hoping to blend
into the background like the new kid who wants
to fit in. If only I could burrow like a mole
feasting on earthworms or grip an ash branch and caw
across the valley. I settle for sitting, my tailbone sore
on this rough-edged stump, my human impeding my animal.

Fifty Finches

Tufts of green grass burst from the lawn
as if someone turned on a grow spigot.
Moss sleeves the bases of bird berry bushes.
After recent rain, the ground's got give.

At the kitchen window, I watch yellowing
finches wade in a feeder full of sunflower seeds.
I've got things to do, but what better way
to spend my time than standing here, counting?

Walking the Dead Furrow

I cross the meadow to walk the path I keep
mowed by the dead furrow. For over thirty
summers it has been filling with shafts of grass,
dead branches and bones of a deer dragged down
by coyotes. Fall rains pooling in Rathbun's fields

crest at the property line and sweep what's light
enough or hasn't rooted into Iron Stirrup Creek.
My first summer on this land, I hired out the disking,
which turned ground that hadn't been harrowed
since the '40s. Field grass and thistle soon took hold

in the smooth dark earth of the dead furrow.
When black-bellied cumulus sidle in from the west,
I take shelter under a white pine and wait, the air
sharp with the tang of liquid manure from a neighbor's
spreader. Rain drops nearly the size of pea gravel pelt

the ground like staggered footfalls. The rhythm lulls
me into a future summer when spittle bugs foam new homes
in the crotches of goldenrod stems, red clover and buttercup
crowd the field and a kid on a landscaping crew weed whacks
grass from my headstone. Whoever lives on this land

may on a walk follow the border yet never know what
happened over decades of seasons, how the furrow
like a buried barometer took the measure of all that ended
here, either folded into soil or swept downhill, the creek
brimming with its cargo, the dead furrow finally filled.

Eucharist

Each April, I pick fiddleheads
in memory of Bill. Bending to slice
the stems of the least unfurled ferns
I cross the hill and back again until
I've filled a colander. It begins raining –
drops on my shoulders add urgency
to how quickly the season will pass.
I retrace my steps along the deer path,
over the fallen white birch, across
the creek's rocks and up to the house
where I hose down the fiddleheads
before going inside to boil water.
Once we welcomed spring this way –
sat knee to knee on a couch,
dipping fiddleheads in a bowl of butter
while back on the hill shadows swelling
with darkness shared the last of the light.

Silent Witnesses

Clouds spread across the Burren, drop low
to the coast, swirl over footpads
of limestone. Wait too long, you'll have
to pick your way back, risk a twisted ankle

or worse. Instead, stay. Let the clouds blanket you
until the calls of sailors blown off course
come clear, when in a past storm the fury opened
enough to let them see their fate and cry out.

Once the storm frees enough light for you
to see your way back, you can carve
another notch in your memory stick, knowing
you got close enough to hear death calling

from the sea, where sailors met their match
just down the way from those who sit under
sheepskin blankets near a fire spitting pitch.
In the evening, the dead return to sit in chairs

saved for them, to witness lives spent on land.
Who knows their thoughts as they listen
to the crack of the fire like the deck splintering
amidship as their brig foundered in a trough,

casting them into the sea to drown
or be bludgeoned by an unforgiving shore.
Too late to exchange their fate, they pull
their blankets closer and nod while listening

to voices whose stories require solid ground
to be told, a fate unfit for those who chose
the sea, whose comfort is the feel of a hull rising
on an open ocean's swells, when the cries

of the last shore birds heading back to the coast fade,
when knotted rigging pulls against cleats
and a following wind fills the sails, snapping the jib
open, the brig surging ahead, all eyes cast forward.

End Game

The name of Professor Marvel's horse
in the *Wizard of Oz* is Sylvester.

It's bad luck to cut a path through
a patch of fiddleheads before they unfurl.

Leave paint on the head of a hammer
and you'll pound your thumb on your next job.

These nuggets stay fixed in my brain
as firmly as barnacles cling to an Atlantic rock.

Yet when I can't recall what my wife told me
yesterday, I despair that my brain is giving up

with a desperate, random efficiency. I fear becoming
the slack-jawed old man whose milky-eyed gaze

can't fix on something across the street
his wife is pointing to with some irritation.

Perhaps he doesn't care, and looks only to satisfy
his obligation, saving his curiosity for later when,

sitting, he'll watch the birds at the feeder,
pleased to make them the focus of his attention,

knowing the way finches swoop toward the seed
and the nuthatch's upside-down walk

are what really count, that after a lifetime of early rising
on others' schedules, now is the time to study

the angle of a pileated woodpecker's head as it strips
bark from an elm trunk, to admire the black mask of a cardinal

or to spend an hour waiting for the Baltimore Oriole
to take a wing-flutter bath under the lawn sprinkler.

I wish for something like this: a perch with a good view
of the feeder and an open window to let the songs in.

Basement Reading

By the time I get home, late afternoon light
silhouettes maple trunks against just-fallen snow.
I bundle groceries in, then troop to the basement
where I crumple newspaper from a bin
to build a fire in the wood furnace.

When a story catches my eye,
I stand on the cold cement floor
in my socks, reading about a Van Gogh
a couple bought for forty-five dollars
at an antique shop, a serial killer who's
sucked away six lives, a border collie
returned home after years on its own,
an old man's sister thought lost in the Holocaust.

Friday arrives before Monday is over,
and I can't tell if the fire in my belly is desire
or too much caffeine. I fill up on others' lives,
time suspended in stories from last week or last year,
depending how far I've reached into the bin.

I hear my wife's car door close.
I hurry to start the fire, balling up lives,
lovers, hundreds of stories left unread.
Paper bursts into flame,
spent coals catch,
fire licks kindling,
a story eager to be told.

Epiphany at Monroe Street Books

Amid the haphazard alphabet
left by browsers searching
for out-of-print titles,
I spend hours cavorting with poets,
standing on the ladder's top rung,
stretching for Lorca and Kumin,
Plath and Bly until,
sated of image and metaphor,
my brain's belly belches
and I sit, resting yet restless,
my choices stacked beside me.

A field mouse with a crust of bread
clamped in its jaw skitters around
the corner and scurries up the side
of a bookcase before dropping
from sight behind Ginsberg.
I imagine that mouse harboring
its crust, returning each night
to eat enough to carry on.

One day I may end like this:
in a dimly lit room smelling of age,
a stack of books at my bedside
for which I'll reach when I need a snack.
After I'm gone, my daughter may
peddle my books at a used book store.
I will rest content knowing
that a mouse in its kingdom
had taken respite behind them.

Too Busy To Sugar

Maple buds bulge at their bases,
tender to the touch. Temperatures
in the twenties at night and forties
by day will set the sap flowing.
I wake from a dream in which
I am treading water in an ocean.
Behind my pounding pulse
I hear in memory the plink-plink-plink
of sap dripping into a tin bucket.

What once I treasured I have traded,
swapped my passions for pursuits
that deliver far less pleasure than
wading knee deep in snow to my stand
of sugar maples to find the right
spots beside ridges of bark to tap.
I'd set the bit, then crank the hand drill
until the milky white flesh of xylem
cycled back along the shaft and fell
into the snow. After tapping the spout
into place, its throat would fill drop
by drop with sap until I'd place my mouth
over the end and drink from the tree.

But not last year, not this year
and probably not next. May I
dream instead that I wade into
March snow and tap the maples?
It would be enough

to hear the sap drop
plink-plink-plink
and to drink my fill:
it would be enough.

The Plow Guy Makes Do

A snowless winter's got Henry up against it.
Keeping a crew busy cutting wood's like tryin'
to fill a sap bucket full of buckshot holes. "Christ,"
he says, "even the Cape's had more snow than us."

His boys are up the notch, slogging through
ankle-high muck. "Shit. Hadta slap the chains
on ennaway to get through it," he says, spitting
in a puddle. "Frick's sake, the mills are at quota!"

Tell Henry the jet stream staying north's causing
this weather and he'll tell you he's got payroll to make
and feet to put into boots and who gives a rat's ass
about what a met'rologist says why we got no snow.

He guesses he'll start tuning up mowers for summer
and give the boys a week or two off. If this weather holds
they'll be cuttin' grass and moppin' sweat come April.
And Henry don't wanna hear no one wishin' for winter.

Norma Stakes Her Claim

When the state finally matched funding from the Feds
for the new bridge over the New Haven River, Norma
waited at the job site for the crew, walked right up
to the super and told him they'd best not put it through
the fiddlehead patch southeast of the crossing point.

"Plenty clear that way," she said, jabbing her thumb.
"I've been pickin' that patch for years. Just so you know."
She turned and walked away. The boys peered out
from sweatshirt hoods pulled tight against the fall cold,
watched Norma's blue skirt shuffle off. "She walks
like a coon," someone mumbled soft enough that
laughter rippled among them, puffing breath clouds.

The bridge went east like Norma wanted. She eyeballed
progress all winter from her Blazer as she crossed
the temporary bridge, window rolled down, parka sleeve
elbowed on the door. She took to waving and after a time
the super would whistle when Norma neared so the crew
was ready to wave when she drove by. In April the boys
were pouring the footings when Norma pulled in to pick
her fiddleheads. She hiked her dress up and one-two'd
over the black plastic staked around the site, short-stepped
over roots and around rocks. The super wasn't about
to tell her she couldn't be there, body like a pear,
stooped over, filling a five-gallon pail most every day.
Close to season's end she brought her grandkids,
who scattered before the super hustled over to tell her
the kids had to go, but then she had him by the hand

and walked him around to see the ferns fanning out.
He looked back at the boys watching them and hollered
they'd best get to work, but they just stood there, helmets
tipped back cocky like they were saying, "You're tellin'
us when Norma's tellin' you?" When the fiddleheads

gave out, Norma stopped stopping and slipped
from the crew's routine. But then one lunch break,
Norma pulled in with a cast iron pot. Soon those big tough
'creters were spooning Norma's fiddlehead stew,
her standing at the head of the line with a ladle and a stack
of colored plastic bowls, the boys nodding how lucky
the state saved her patch. Before afternoon break the super
saw her Blazer, so he hollered and the boys got ready to wave,
but it was a look-alike. You should've seen their faces
when they realized it wasn't Norma.

Mettle and Pluck

Below hills gloved by clouds,
white bird berries beckon fall
into the valley. Top-heavy
goldenrod leans over apples
mashed flat by the lawn mower,
yellow jackets gorging on the pulped
white flesh, abdomens wriggling.
Geese vee south. I crane my neck
to watch their freefall toward where
after too many winters we wish
we were bound, even before colors march
down the mountains and beaver gather enough
saplings to tide them over. Cold seeps
into cracks we meant to seal last summer.
Our house fills with the scent of cedar
and mothballs as coats come out of storage
and we reclaim gloves gladly cast aside
last April. When winter powers into our lives
we will welcome it at first, reveling in snow
whose cover should obscure regrets
amassed from other seasons but which
magnifies instead, insistent we acknowledge
them before getting the shovel from the shed
and start clearing from the head of the path.

2. Letting Go

Change is nature's delight.

Marcus Aurelius

Ever Spring
For Amelia

Maple sap reached a rolling boil,
moisture steamed windows, wafted
upstairs to my daughter's bedroom
where she lay before sleep, inhaling
the sweet scent of the season.

The spring she came into her own,
she leaned shirtless over a stairway railing,
saying how she loved smelling the sap.
I avoided looking at the nubs of her breasts
so she wouldn't be self-conscious, a father's
futile attempt to slow her turn to adolescence.

Every spring snow melts
in a near-perfect circle
around the base of each maple.
Trunks breathe again, growing
toward the memory of opening
buds that will stop the flow of sap.

I stand by the stove,
waiting for the moment
when sap turns to syrup,
capturing the last of the season.

Farewell, Second Summer

On a warm, cloudless, mid-October day,
a friend exclaimed, "It's Second Summer!"
I explained that Second Summer arrives
in November, only after a killing frost, on a day
when the temperature rises into the low 40s.
But people have forgotten or, worse, never knew.

It matters no more. A warming planet
has sent Second Summer the way of the dodo
and the '57 Chevy. But I remember
those November days when I inhaled deep
into my lungs air sweet with a hint of rotted leaves,
a dash of water from the creek, a pinch
of earth from garden soil thawing, and just
for a minute these would mix into early May
with crocus and iris tips inching upward
and the bellies of maple buds swelling.

Maybe I'll live long enough to see
Second Summer return. I'll strip
down to my tee-shirt and walk around
full of piss and vinegar like the young buck
who asks his favorite girl to the movies,
suspended in that moment when he's not sure
if she'll say yes but for craziness not caring
if it's no. However it goes, he'll know he stood
at the edge and leaned out far enough to get a good view.

Another Time

For my sister, Emily

Another time, we'll walk the paths I take mornings
with the dogs: crossing the field, we'll stop at patches
of birdfoot violets whose blue matches sky above
the ridgeline. We'll delight in dutchman's breeches,
snowdrops and oxeye daisies. I'll piggy-back-ride you
across a beaver-dammed stream so your city boots
won't get mucked by Vermont mud. Another time,
when you can visit longer, we'll hear the courting
chortle of wild turkeys' in Rathbun's field, such a fuss.
We'll sight coltsfoot by the creek. Stepping on grass
tufts, we'll cross wetland where behind a row of cedars
we'll pick marsh marigolds for the table. Another time,
cued by the raspy notes of the phoebe, we'll strain
to catch a glimpse of its gray breast in white pine
branches chucked about by a south wind. After
you've gone – when marigold pollen rings the vase
base in a precise circle – I'll stand on a rise in the field
and imagine us admiring something I can't see from here.

Burying the Clan

My aunts and uncles are dying
one by one, the family's longevity
unraveling. Gareth got brain cancer,
Bob, bladder cancer, Cynthia,
leukemia. Today we meet in this town
of unfamiliar streets for my aunt, Debby.
Speakers drone on the way they do
and I drift off, imagine the departed
gathering above the family beach
in Manomet, each agreeing that Cynthia
has captured the brown of the bluff precisely
in her watercolor. Taking the wooden stairs
between Cape Cod rose and prickly pear,
the dead shed their clothes on the beach, swim
between rocks named Symplegades and cross
the Bay till the tip of the Cape corrals them.
They carve and swallow the moon, spit pieces of it
back on the beach for a walker to wonder at brightness found.

Sitting in Half Light

For Sparky

My old dog lies
at my feet. His dark
mass on the floor calls me
to kneel by him, rub his side.
He rolls to his back.
As I slide my hand along
his rib cage, he moans,
deep and guttural.
I lift his ear and whisper into it;
his wide, fluffy tail flaps,
each downward stroke
marking time on the floor,
his world taking shape
at the sound of my voice.

The Pie Man Retires

How I will miss the rise of his pies,
the crossed pattern of fork tines
on crust's edge, how he sweetened
just enough that the berries ruled

a world to which I fully gave
my palate, swooning for fresh
fruits' seduction in all seasons,
now wishing I'd had one more taste

before he tossed his last apron
into the hamper. No more pinched-pink
cheeks dusted with flour or shirt sleeves
mottled by plump blueberries' juices.

Did he take his pie crust secrets
with him? Does his Rolodex of recipes
now stock his pantry shelf at home?
Even as I shrug an admission that

his successor's pies could be as good,
I doubt he'll have the cheeks, the flour-flecked
apron, or the glint in his eye as he fits inside
an oven others would think full just one more pie.

Ginny's Leaving
For Dave Avery

The beach is crowded with family
in their orange, teal and blue coats
stark against pale brown Manomet bluffs,
talking, laughing, catching up
at our annual day-after-Thanksgiving picnic.

High-tide breakers rolling onto the pebbled beach
make it hard to hear conversations with a small
group of my cousins, so we huddle closer,
our nostrils full of the sharp scent of salt
and seaweed, wind tunneling into our ears.

We turn our heads toward a figure monkish
under a hooded green sweatshirt. She scuffs
divots in the sand as her husband walks her over.
The breeze catches her hood and peels it back.
She bows her head, looking at the sand.

"Hi, Ginny," I say. "I'm Warren, Laurie's boy."
"Laurie's boy," she whispers back.
"Laurie Green's boy," I try again,
as if my mother's maiden name
might fuse a synapse, but her eyes glaze

as she looks to the side, as if seeing something
far away. Awkward clings in my throat.
"It's nice to see you, Ginny," I say,
taking her hand. She squeezes my fingers
the way fish nibble toes in shallow water.

Dave moves her to the next group. As Ginny
soft-steps away, my cousins and I cast glances
at each other as if we're about to share a secret.
But we pick up again, trading stories from our lives
and sharing memories of summers ago.

I hold a hope that Ginny remembers setting up
her easel with my late aunt Cynthia beside marshes
and cranberry bogs, barns and salt flats, painting
the watercolors now so prized by my family,
but Ginny has faded further than last year.

Days later, in a windowless meeting
room, trying to listen as a colleague
drones on, scanning how much
of the agenda we still have to cover,
I realize that I never said goodbye.

A Soldier's Story

For veterans in their longest battle

Over the years I'd heard the old man holler strings
of swears from the house when buying hay for my hens.
His son told me how his father was in the first wave
at Omaha Beach, saw buddies he'd foxholed
with at Salerno diced by the MG42s bunkered
on the cliff, his face tattooed in blood pumping
from severed limbs twitching on the LCA's floor
before those who still had legs hit the surf and by God's
dumb luck made it to a beachhead but were pinned until
a private humped up with a bazooka and took out the gunner.

When he pulled a shotgun on his wife and set
the milking parlor on fire, his son shipped him
to the vet's home where he died among other old soldiers
who started fist fights, pissed their beds, and woke screaming.

They painted the house and trim so the place looked new.
Some evenings his widow's on the porch watching
the Green Mountains rose over from an Adirondack sunset,
about when sounds begin building in the marsh, chirps
and chug-ups rising from cool, still, black water
and her grandson home from work starts nailing
sheathing on his new barn, the thwack-thwack-thwack
of the hammer adding to the rhythm that pulses long
after last light, building like an incoming tide.

I imagine the old man pulling into the dooryard in a '46 Ford
he bought from Foster's with milk checks they'd saved,

him flush with luck and no worries beyond fixing the tedder
before fall. No sign then that his new-born son would
find him shouting both sides of a conversation,
cringe when his temper erupted at seemingly
nothing while loading furnace wood into a wheelbarrow.

Hard to believe any of that's possible when sun beads
dew sweat down the side of the barn and steam's
rising off the manure pile and the cows' bags are full
and the pump's purring and the sharp tang of manure
cleans clogged sinuses and milk prices are up so it seems
to take less time to muck the stalls and flush the gutters.

When I stop in afternoons for a couple bales his son and I
talk pick-up trucks while he wipes teats clean and spreads
fresh hay to keep the girls occupied. Through clouds
of sweet Timothy dust I imagine the old man moving
his milking stool bag to bag, hear the skreak of milk
against the bottom of the bucket, the sound growing
fuller with foaming milk as the bucket fills, the pulse
building till it synchs with sounds rising at the end
of the day from cool, black water pulsing in the marsh
like waves on the beach, blood in the old man's veins.

A Walk with Uncle Gareth

He slurs his words
when I call to wish him well
with his chemotherapy.

He's still confident he will take me
for a cruise in his new Chris Craft
with its gleaming mahogany deck.

Years ago at a family reunion
we each went walking in Holmes Field
and came upon the other on a knoll.

Strolling the rolling hills that glaciers
carved, we admired the cranberry bogs.
He predicted the cirrus clouds forecast rain.

I hold in memory a picture
of us wandering in that field.
Gareth is pointing, his arm

traces the lay of the land, the late
August sun claiming the gesture –
the only time I was alone with him.

Josephine's Directions

Mopping her brow of New Orleans humidity,
she thanks me for letting an old woman who wandered
by sit at my table under the restaurant's umbrella.

"Mercy! Be a long, hot summer. Glad I ain't
gonna be here to sweat through it."

She eyes me eating gumbo, which I say is good.
Smiling, her gold tooth flashes. "Oh, honey, that's
French Market gumbo. Here's how you make real gumbo:

In a heavy-bottom pan make a roux good and dark,
then add your onion, bell peppers and celery.

She was living in Houston, and liked it, but
moved back to New Orleans for family. She's
moving again. "Too much evil here after Katrina."

Gotta bake your chicken. That's key to good gumbo.
You can't boil it! Gotta lotta flavor in those bones.

She'll be moving to New York next month, where
her sister lives. "I just want to settle in one place
where I can stay. I don't see that's too much to ask."

Stir your spices into the roux – add lots of garlic –
and let 'em simmer. Then add your chicken and sausage.

Her gold-tooth bobbing, she says no when I offer
to buy her a glass of lemonade, that I've been
kind enough to let her sit and rest in the shade.

*Cover all of it with your stock and let it simmer. In the last
fifteen minutes, add the shrimp so you don't overcook it.*

She smooths a fold in her print dress. "I guess I'll miss
it some here. Nice place to visit." She laughs, standing
to leave. Seeing me about to ask another question, she says

"Just bring out your pots and start cookin',
honey. See what happens. You'll be fine."

Letting Go
For Amelia

When you were nine, after you saw that
I would be good to your mother, you let me
hold your hand when we ambled through town.

I said nothing about how thrilled I was –
I didn't want to hurry the day when you
would let me know that you'd grown beyond it.

Had I told you of my concern, you would have assured me
that it would not be so. But one day, perhaps weeks later,
when I took your hand, you gently pulled it back.

Now we meet for lunch and discuss where you walked
the dog last night, where you're planning a getaway,
a TV show both of us watched, or the trouble with Congress.

I know this, too, will not last – that in time you may
move again beyond my hand that now holds
the door for you or lifts to wave as we part

and head back toward our workplaces. You do not know
I turn to watch you, marveling at who you have become
or that, when you step from the curb, I catch my breath.

3. Taking Your Turn

Poems in memoriam

The life of the dead is set in the memory of the living.
Cicero

Dublin Symphony

From this rise in the road, terracotta chimney pots
of all heights and breadths spire the view. I wonder:
Which would be yours? And how would I tell?
Does each whistle in a different tone like many lips blowing
across bottle tops? And what would the timbre of each
be for the stages of your long life? Some low and mournful,
others soaring and joyous, but most with slight variations
that echo the rise and fall of your days. Would each sound
differently among the seasons? Depending on wind direction,
some might pitch higher, some deeper, but each resonant
with notes closest to yearning and wonder. Would your
chimney pot be the one where the seagull rests before flying
back to the coast? Or the one whose top is fluted
like a church organ pipe? Or that octangular with intricate
scroll work? I think, instead, yours would be the one
with the grasses growing from a chimney no longer used.
Yes, surely yours. And though I can't tell from here,
no doubt yours shelters a nest of swallows whose taut flights
weave among the chimney pots, their shrill cries
joining the symphony of whistles for those whose
ears are tuned to the music that crescendos, arcing across
these gray, slate rooftops before they sweep out to sea.

Laurie Baker

Opening Day

1.
It's opening day in heaven.
Bill loads his gear into the pick-up,
calls his golden retriever, Taffy,
and drives to a bend in the creek
where rocks have been worn round
by eons of spring flooding.

It's opening day in heaven.
You might think the fishing's easy,
that brookies would jump into the net,
but trout in heaven are just as smart –
the fly won't attract any
until you use your wits.

Cool air settling on ground
warm from yesterday's sun
sets steam rising where snow is still
ankle-deep in east-facing swales.
Bill says something to the dog,
steps into the water and casts.

2.
Twenty years ago Bill knocked
on my door early evening in mid-January
with Taffy dead on a plastic snow sled –
he'd once asked if he could bury her
on the land. With no need to speak,
I pulled on my boots and a jacket

then got a pick and shovel. We walked
to a spot in the field where he said,
She can see everything from here.
He took the pick, cleaved cracks
in the frozen ground, turning away my help,
wanting only his mark on the old dog's grave.

I held the flashlight as he broke through
the frost line, then shoveled dirt into a pile.
Plumes of breath swirled about him
as he hunched over the deepening hole.
After we lowered Taffy in, he turned
earth back over her and set the stone.

3.
Panic edged his wife's voice –
Bill had gone to the hospital with chest pains
and while waiting for a doctor had keeled over
backward. By the time I got there, he
was respirated, his chest rising and falling,
beeps marking a rhythm not his own.

Doctors thought brain damage
because he'd been without oxygen.
Rachel waited bedside two weeks for him
to wake, hoping that the man who had brought her
coffee in bed each morning and nuzzled her ear
would return as quickly as he'd left.

When they moved him to the ICU,
Rachel okayed pulling the tubes.
Bill breathed for two more days.
When he frothed at the mouth,
we watched his chest fall.
Rachel caught her breath.

4.
When last winter broke, I realized
that Taffy's stone had long since sunk
and been covered by sod. I poked
with a pitchfork until I found it,
peeled the grass back, air thick
with the scent of dirt, the stone as he'd set it.

Each spring I welcome the signs that mark opening day:
maple buds swelling, fiddleheads about to unfurl,
the dust-broom brown of fields, marsh marigolds
tinting swamps yellow, gray fuzz on hills,
Bill standing behind his beat-up truck,
back hunched as he ties a fly to the line.

The trout are biting in heaven.
Bill has three nice brookies in his basket.
Taffy's gotten into some pucker brush and burrs;
Bill shakes his head at the thought of untangling them.
He starts the truck, watches the light play in a birch,
his favorite spot to sit and remember.

                                        Bill Dart

Missing

Her friends watched her front walk for three weeks
before hunters tracking a buck uncovered her body
buried under brush. Who would wrest life from this
widow who camped, kayaked, hooked rugs
and helped her neighbors without credit or thanks?

What would fill the hole in the hearts of those
unknowns who hauled her from her Sheffield home?
Her children have pain to spare that could fill
a ventricle. Her friends might portion their plenty
of grief to displace space in an auricle.

The police could fill the atria by converting
tight-lipped retorts to explanations when reporters
ask for progress in the year-old case. But not
enough to offset her killers' urge to break bones
brittle as early winter wafer ice, ignore the voice

brimming with pain, slough off pleas for mercy.
They wake each morning holding her final twitch
in their hands, turn from the mirror and walk among us.
Once caught, we'll watch them in shackles shuffle
into court, search their faces for clues unanswered
by media reports, take the measure of the hearts
in whose chambers her last breath floats
like an incomplete rhyme, the comeback that arrives
long after, the gesture seen too late to return,
the wish to cross off one last item on the list.

Pat O'Hagan

Voice on the Phone

I recall our last conversation
from 30 years ago in the way
one remembers a dream:
fuzzy, fading, far away.

You said you were hoping
for the best, but your voice
cracking told me the lump
in your armpit had staked its claim.

Once while visiting, I got up early.
Shuffling to the bathroom, I came upon
you and Marion lying on the living room rug.
You were locked in a kiss, the kind borne
of longing and devotion so deep
you didn't know I was there.

I mark the years by what never happened –
your graduation from law school,
yours and Marion's wedding,
our trips to see the Phillies play,
the Mercedes 250 SL you always wanted,
stories we would have shared.

When morning light filtering through curtains
casts long shadows into Marion's living room,
she still may whisper your name.

D. Bruce Bowie

Interim

Bunny's sudden death has drawn the family to Lowell.
I stand in her living room while her husband and daughters,
huddled in the kitchen, discuss funeral arrangements,
their voices blending with the refrigerator motor's hum.
Here is a watercolor of a landscape propped on an easel –
birch, rocks, the foreground blurred from snow-melt steam
rising on a warm early spring day. Here a paint-splotched
step ladder turned bookcase, ferns in green and brown pots,
a mirror reflecting a fichus fig, silver-painted radiators.
Sunlight casts mullion shadows above a pale white throw
on a red-flowered ottoman. A plush couch pillow holds
its last impression as if Bunny, impatient for a conversation
to end, rose and walked into the watercolor. She steps over
a stone wall and strolls among birch down to the river.

Barbara Fairbank

Testament

Stones on the old dog's grave sink.
Not enough to notice in passing but
gradual enough one day to surprise.
In the early years after he died, I planted
marigolds, but then got too busy, though
each time I pass I pull weeds and apologize.

Stones on the old dog's grave sink –
long after the blanket in which I wrapped
him rotted, long after flesh and fur fell
from bone, long after I stood above freshly
shoveled soil and wept, the stones I stacked
are slipping as the earth reclaims its own.

Stones on the old dog's grave sink –
Tempted to restack them, I resolve
instead to plant marigolds so the next time
I pass he'll show a full splay of colors,
which won't stop the slide, but for the rest
of summer might convince me I can slow it down.

                              Rusty the Corgi

Water Borne

John rows out of Tanner's Cove,
head tipped forward on his long neck,
eyes gripping a bird on shore.
As a younger man with keener sight,
he would have known the bird by its body.
Now he waits for flight to name the shape.
When it bursts from a yellow pine, he knows
from the short, rounded wings and dark,
hooked beak that it's a Sharp Shinned Hawk.

Oars ripple water. He pauses between strokes –
drops running from each blade string
necklaces of concentric circles in his wake.
The feel of water under a keel
is as comfortable as a lover's hand
while walking. From a spit of land
a couple watches him row. It is dusk.
They speak in hushed tones he can barely hear.
He ships his oars and glides.

John Clarke

Discovery at Manomet

She got her gift from her grandmother
who painted marshes and haystacks
in Holland. With palette and easel
Cynthia, wearing colored smock and straw hat,
spent hours in the woods with whippoorwills
and bob whites. She plied the bluffs, scrub brush
and pitch pines between the cranberry bogs
at Holmes Farm and the coast just shy of Cape Cod.

Years later at the family summer house
I found a stack of her watercolors.
Spreading them out on a bed, instantly
I was transported to trails between brambles
and sumac and to the bluffs when the tide
turns before inching back up boulders
the color of sparrow feathers. I imagined
sitting in the shade behind her as she painted
the weathered red cottage on the far side
of Skokes Pond, felt how calloused our feet
would have been if we'd walked shoeless
months of mornings along sandy coastal paths.

When I asked if I could have one or two,
she insisted I take all, that she'd forgotten about them.
Hung in my home now, these watercolors recall
a life unfettered by husband and children,

car repairs, a mortgage, and what to make for dinner.
Then, her choices were which greens to mix
to capture afternoon light in a hemlock,
whether to take the path by the Weeks house
or follow the high-crowned dirt road east to the beach.

Cynthia chose to be buried in Manomet,
close to the trails she'd walked,
now overgrown as though they'd never been.
Each time I return to the summer house
everything seems smaller, the paths shorter,
the boulders at the beach less massive.
Yet when I look to the top of the bluffs,
I see Cynthia sitting at her easel,
watching a gull catch an updraft –
after a few strokes, it flies onto the paper.

Cynthia Joy Green Platt

Making Beach Plum Jelly

In a flowered lavender hat bleached
from years of walking the wrack line,
Aunt Helen led me between sections of snow
fence lining the shoreward side of a sand dune.
It's familiar ground, so she knew where
the beach plum bushes were. *Not many left.*

We walked the gray sand of Duxbury Beach
until she turned behind a dune identical
to the rest and led me to a beach plum bush
clustered with purple fruits. *It's a shame
how storms take a toll on these gorgeous dunes
and just whisk away the beach plums.* She flicked
her wrist as if brushing a bee from her sleeve.

As I picked, the chalky bloom filled my fingerprints.
She explained the steps to make the jelly, that
while the new batch cooled we'd sit at her kitchen
table, enjoy what's left of last year's crop on toasted
homemade bread with mint from her garden in our tea.
She'd tell me stories about her parents
who came from Brookline to the beaches
just north of Cape Cod with their brood of nine.

In early September sun, with an Atlantic breeze
light on our necks, our satchels filled with plums.
After we picked the ripe fruit, she looked
down the shoreline, pointed toward another
stand of bushes and said, *No time to lose.*

Helen Lincoln Fowler

Regret

After two spinal fusions your back stayed hunched
for as long as you lived, the old bones without
give, too much for the pounding you would have taken
riding in my skiff to the southern part of Lake Champlain
that narrows toward the locks at Whitehall – where
I said I would take you but never did. Instead, we sat
in your living room, sipped tea and made small talk.
I could not bear to describe the beauty you missed:
how marsh grasses lifted in the wake with such grace
I felt the pull on their roots like someone coaxing me
toward a place I had never been; how the channel twisted,
unfolding each new view; about the arc of a crane's wings
lifting from a clam-strewn strip of sand, the sharp rise
of rocks on the New York side, how fish broke. We'd
have stopped for lunch, pulled the boat against Pulpit
Rock and sat on top eating sandwiches, watching
breezes ripple through river birch and black alder
before we pushed off and headed south.

Horace Baker

Taking Your Turn

Bernie died in winter after cancer
called and confined those old bones
to a bed on the back side of the house.
He had a view of snow drifted
on the garage roof that last year
he would have pulled down with a snow rake.

His jowl-creased face rested on a pillow,
his hair now curling over his ears.
When I teased him about it, he said,
"Don't want to pay twice! Why pay
for a haircut now when 'afore long
the undertaker'll get paid to do it?"

We traded pleasantries, and he thanked me
for coming. Leaning over, I kissed his cheek,
felt the bristle of stiff white whiskers
on his unevenly shaven face, and began
the awkward exit, turning for a last look
in my lead-foot shuffle from the room.

At the reception, friends took turns
strumming tunes, believing that one day
they would sit in a circle in heaven
and pass the guitar, each choosing a song,
except for God, who, Bernie would tell them
on the sly, doesn't sing and only plays banjo.

                              Bernie Martin

4. Harvest

Poems for Sharon

Be blown on by all the winds.
            Henry David Thoreau

Unwritten Novel

Our story would read
like Vermont hills
under light snow,
just enough white
to reveal the ragged edges
of rocks and ledges.

Our story would read
like a water lane threading
through marsh grass
switching in a tidal flat
that loops back on itself
until it opens onto ocean.

Your elbow bends,
a heel barely rising
as you water a violet,
then set down the watering can
as if in answer to my prayer
for paper and pen.

Memory of Touch

Wind rattles windowpanes.
Birch branches rake the roof.
Shed door slapping, fit to snap
its hinges. My feet on rough dirt,
I walk naked in darkness, slip latch
through strike, brace the door
with a fallen limb. Wind coats
my skin. Tree crowns thrash
in half-moon light. I picture you
turning in your sleep, blanket
falling away from your breasts,
then thread the path back to bed.

Morning Serenade

Darling, I have woken before you,
drawn from sleep by your delicate
snores. You sound like a French horn
with a mission to round the edges
of a rough dream. But then you roll
over on your side and continue,
your snoring now close to an oboe.
I lean back against the pillow,
imagining a symphony of snores
to which I have a front-row seat.
Your body heat embers beside me.
I pull the blanket up to my chin, closing
my eyes, your snore serenade drifting me
off to a dream in which I've been asked
to guest-conduct. At the rostrum, I tap
my baton, reminding the renegade trumpets
to play their adagio soothingly while asking
the impetuous wood section to stop talking
trash about the tuba players so we may hear
the solo the French horn has been practicing.

Opening

I crease each
page of a new
book back
against the binding,
starting
with the first
then the last,
like kissing
your upper lip
then your lower,
my tongue exploring
the delicate line of your neck,
running my finger
along the binding,
your arcing spine's ridge,
each page
one by one
your nipples blooming,
the sweet scent of fresh
paper pungent as each
page turns
opening
opening.

Somewhere

Thunderheads glide east –
sun breaks through west.
Rain rappels leaf to leaf,
applause for the show just ended,
which rumbles its curtain call
from the other side of the mountain.
Disappointed at no rainbow, I imagine
colors so sharp I could pin pictures
to them. Home from work, you ask
if there was a rainbow. I describe
the purple first, your favorite color.

Unfurling

Fiddleheads thrust through matted leaves,
insistent on their share of light.
We pick a panful before they unfurl,
brush the parchment-thin brown sheaths
from their heads in a sink of cold water,
then double-boil, the secret of turning bitter to sweet.

We melt butter in a bowl,
sit thigh to thigh on the couch –
drops drip down the green stems
before we bite, the flavor delicate
as the scent of spring air slipping
in through a cracked window.

Peeling off our clothes,
burrowing under the covers,
touching each other's winter white skin
with fingertips calloused from feeding
firewood to furnace,
we unfurl our lush greenery.

Harvest

The furnace fan
kicks into gear
for the first time
since late spring –
heating duct dust
scratches our nostrils.

The cat curls
into a blanket
on the couch,
gnawing a burr
from her back.

The light of a full moon
funnels our breath into plumes
as we walk to the garden
through dew-heavy grass
to admire sunflowers'
heavy-seeded heads.

Cold hardens onions,
potatoes cry out
to be dug.
We go upstairs
to lie in bed
pore to pore,
putting ourselves up
for another winter.

5. Lay of the Land

We are what we are given and what is taken away.
Wendell Berry

Losing the Cranberry Bogs
For Galen Green

Galen stands on a hill overlooking cranberry bogs
that have been next door to his family home for most
of a century. From the east, wind carries the scent
of seaweed baking in late August sun, the pounding
of surf on boulders at Platt Beach and the screech of gulls
squabbling over blue crabs seeking cover in the wrack line.

Horace Holmes farmed these bogs for forty years.
After he died, an organic farmer tried his hand.
Galen agreed to mow the brambles and bittersweet
back from the bogs until the farmer got his footing,
but the bottom fell out of the market.
Now weeds and grasses have free reign.

Taking the tire-worn road back to the barn,
Galen peers through a window crusty with sea salt,
sees on floor planks patches of motor oil like age spots
dropped from the engine of the Model-T truck that once
hauled crates of cranberries in to be sorted. His nostrils
fill with the dry, dusty scent of cedar shakes in full sun.

Galen follows the grass path up to the house. Looking back,
he scans the roll of a hill down to one of the bogs where
    heat shimmers above the stubble of red and green cranberry
vines.
    He remembers himself as a gangly teen in a white t-shirt,
flying a brown box kite from the knoll. In his wrists
he still feels the tug of the kite shooting upward in a stiff

breeze.

Coming in for lunch, he'd find bread
in a basket and a plate of softening butter
on the metal-top table, early Macs drip-drying
in the dish drain. His mother would enter quietly,
strands of her hair askew from the breeze.
"Galen," she'd ask. "How are the cranberries?"

Laying Claim

Beavers dammed the creek
that, once diverted, washed enough
earth downstream to undermine
my neighbor's barbed wire fence
which he had to move to keep
his cows from crossing. He's angry
at land lost at his expense.
With no reason to blame the beaver's
calling, my only want was
to return the creek to run its course.
This took a shovel, sheets of tin
and 2x4s hatcheted into stakes.

To learn how long a creek has traced
its course, count the turns it takes.
This water, then, has passed this place
for many years. For my rerouting,
should I subtract one turn not taken?
Most days I yield to forces beyond
my sway, but this time I intervened
to return water to where it once flowed,
insistent on meeting my obligation
to maintain the boundary, knowing that
my neighbor, if he chose, could return
the fence to where it once stood.

Getting started proved easy.
Water, quick to follow my lead,
filled mud channels I fashioned

from clods of clay-fused soil.
The last trickles proved hardest
to redirect. Water found its way
around the soil quick as I plopped
it in place, leaving me sweat-drenched
in late July sun. When at last the creek
reclaimed its path, it seeped at first
before its track widened. With stakes
behind tin sheets I rebuilt the bank.

A new brood of beaver one day
will lodge here, build a dam,
divert the creek again, which, deep in memory,
may recall when it was forced to follow
a different path. If I returned, I'd marvel
at each direction since taken, wonder
what became of soil washed downstream
when spring rains crested, swept across fields,
retrieving land to which they staked a rightful claim.

Preparation

Grass tips roil on the hill
unlike in wind from the west
when stems bend in unison.
Tree tops tip me off, too,
crowns flailing the news.

When the cloud bank crosses
the ridge I move inside,
feel the force of wind and rain
that yesterday drove through
a quarter-inch crack in a window,
staining a century-old pen and ink
drawn by my great-great grandmother.

How long would I last if I lived
without walls or roof, had to fend
for myself? What would I choose
to take with me for my life outside?

I resist temptation to turn on a light
as the storm pushes dusk across the field.
When thunder opens its doors, I start a list.

Surveying the Boundary

Winter opens woods, lets me see through tangles
of barberry that wrap the world of the wren,
leads me to a cellar hole filled with leaves, branches,
shards of clay pots and a tin can with just a letter of label left.

I imagine the lives of those who lived here where earth covets
the weight of crumbling walls whose rocks strained farmers'
backs, clearing the land with crowbars and ropes tied to oxen
yoke to make room for this foundation now settling into its ruin.

Just so on my own land, one season lying fallow
would see sumac, goldenrod and bird berry begin
to reverse years of clearing. Just so would my garden
be overrun by hedge mustard and creeping charlie.

Standing inside this crumble of house, I scan the ridge line
of gray stone, imagine how the view was different for those
who first settled here on land now overrun by maple
and ash, how they marked the change of seasons when winter

lost its bite and spring found titmice scratching through
brittle maple leaves by the back door. What I grow and clear
on my own land marks the boundary to which
I lay claim, which inspires brambles and sumac
to repossess, cycling me back to questions I first asked
How much to clear? How big the garden?
I pocket the tin can to remind me
that I cannot hold no matter how firmly I grip.

The Fate of Faith

The history of a building is the life of those who lived in it.

Only walls remain in this 18th century stone church
near Kinvara, wood rafters long-since fallen
where its congregation once knelt,
where town folk asked God to muster forces
greater than they to bring in a good crop,
heal the sick or ease lambing season.

"What happened to the pews?" must be a common wonder.
Before the rafters gave way, perhaps the faithful made
space in their homes and mudrooms, each pew then a relic
before which they'd once knelt, above which they'd stood
like the roof that sheltered them from Irish winds
until decay became as inevitable as days'-long rain.

And what of those in whose hearts faith rested?
Needing another roof to shelter belief, they carried theirs
to another church like a satchel stuffed with a fine crop
of parsnips and potatoes, even while knowing that memories
of them would fade as generations passed, like old tubers
hoed under in soil turned for next season's crop.

Underfoot, chips of slate on the stone floor scatter,
reminders of the certainty that once stood here. Weeds
and grasses grow among the stones, harbingers
of another season, faith appearing where it's least likely
to find shelter, to gain a foothold where it needs no marker
to stake its claim among the living who happen here.

After the Beach
for Dwight and Joyce

Shells shaped by tides
and ground by sand
speak to us in ways
we cannot define
when we select which
to lift and scrutinize,
which to pocket and take home,
unwrap and place on a bureau
or kitchen shelf, and which long
after still appeal among other shells
and stones we've accumulated
in a cache of things significant
which we often stop to admire
even though we can't recall
what impelled us once to choose them.

Inventory, January 1, 2015

Cold brittles lichen stubble on a stone wall.
Snow dusts grass tufts under a cedar's canopy
like shadows at dusk. I could curl on a mat
of browning needles around the trunk of a white
pine and dream that I'll be remembered after
the house in which I raised my daughter hosts
new owners and I fade in the clutter of her
not-yet-born children's memories. Here is what I know:
after two nights below zero, the creek will freeze.
When a maple trunk cracks, the earth shudders
in the balls of my feet. Rime frost rims the end
of a beech leaf with teeth so precise I must be
at nose length to see the jagged edge. Cold
seeping from coat through shirt to tug at bone
is enough to begin this new year. I stand in wind
shuttling up the valley. Three chickadees peck
for seeds at the base of an oak. The instant I look
away, they scatter, leaving a whirr of wings.

Claiming the Land

Claude Anderson's given it up, MLS sign
hammered in by the mailbox, kids gone
to straphang on the MTA, unwilling
to be in bed by 8:00 and up at 4:00 or ride
the price of milk low to high and down again.

Weeds he clipped from the sides
of the barn that leaned east for years
cover the base of the siding:
rot's not far behind. Rust
patches the milking shed roof.

Ivy climbs front porch posts,
threads a downspout, up unpainted
clapboards, fingerlings climb to chinked
shingles. Maple branches droop enough
to take a seat in their own shade.

Someone looking to graze alpacas
might find a home here, or if the market
turns, a developer could take a chance:
capes on a cul de sac or rows of ranches.
A sculptor could convert the shed

to a studio, cut a skylight to see Lincoln Hill
turn purple like it did late afternoons when
Claude finished mucking stalls, flushing gutters,
and Doris, stirring stew, heard his boots
crunch on gravel by the back porch.

Squatter's Rights at Iron Stirrup Creek

While walking the dogs, I spy the calling cards
of a new beaver colony: bark and cambium chips
scattered like dice around the trunk of a birch
tell the story of several incisors working late.

All summer those beavers build several dams,
stripping the land of high-bush cranberry, alders
and clusters of black birch with trunks the size of wrists.

They angle four-inch thick branches into creek banks
to buttress the dams' bases, weave hundreds of sticks
to build bulk. Then with raspberry canes and clumps
of beard grass dug by the roots, they seal holes,
using their tails to spread river mud like black butter.

When I first moved here, I lay awake, imagining them
stripping the land. Thirty years and three colonies later,
I stand still by a woodpecker-pocked elm trunk
at dusk, waiting for the first beaver to appear.
Its head splits the water up the middle of the creek.
A second surfaces; their paths crisscross.
When I turn to leave, they slap their tails: a warning,
sure, but they're really bidding me good night.

When wind wails through bare maples
and the temperature drops to 10 below,
I'll huddle under blankets, worrying about pipes
freezing and if I have enough furnace wood
while the beavers feed on birch stockpiled beneath the ice,

their lodge's air moist, primal, ready for kits come April
when the dogs and I will stroll down to see what's new.

Hilltop Cycle
For Dwight Fowler

This white pine with a two-arms-
around-the-circumference trunk
snapped in half just like that
in wind that raged through the valley.
Dwight and I dab at the still-sticky sap.

Black birch lie side by side
in precise symmetry. Dwight says
it's like a giant sending
us a message by setting them so.

A cherry's ragged, upturned roots
spread like broken lifelines
gripping rocks big as fists.

Earth's story reads like this:
sandy loam atop layers of clay
hardening here since glaciers
dropped gravel and rounded mountains.

With his forefinger, Dwight traces
swirls on a white ash's trunk,
an unknown alphabet, the latest entry
in the cycle toward a hardwood forest.

We sense motion deep in the earth
as the story catches up to us,
tightening tendons in our necks.

Aging in Place

Half the roof is gone.
The remaining rafters
like a back stooped
from a life of labor
sag under the weight
of slate installed in the '40s
when Bristol boys just home
from the war raised this barn.

Into the tie stalls where Jerseys
once gave milk with the highest
butterfat count in the valley,
slates like rotted teeth slip
one by one to the concrete,
chipping and cracking.

Soon the gable wall that's been leaning
for months will collapse, the ridge pole
will fall; then, the cupola will topple
into the milking parlor. The girt
spanning the double doors
will splinter like a broken forearm.

Across the road from the barn,
in the bedroom at the back
of the house, one light burns.
The old farmer nods to re-runs
of the Lawrence Welk show,
his dentures soaking
beside him in a shallow glass.

Farm Widow

She rises early,
turns on a table lamp.
Light through its blue shade
and a yellowed curtain
fills a window
with a sallow pallor.

She trusts habit.
Even after her husband's heart
seized, even after she'd sold
the Holsteins, even after snow
on slate caved in the barn's roof,
she still gets up before the birds.

She welcomes light.
Settled in his armchair, she looks
up from her knitting needles,
watches sun flood the field,
corn stalk stubble casting
shadows the length of fingers.

She remembers touch.
His worn brown jacket
crusty with sweat,
the calluses on his hands
thick as pads on a cat's foot,
his palms cradling her breasts.

The day opens.

She turns off the lamp,
shuffles into the kitchen.
Lifting the iron skillet,
she begins to make breakfast,
not yet hungry.

Lay of the Land

For Vermont dairy farmers, who carry on

I used to go by George's barn at milking time,
take in the deep scent of silage and the sharp
sting of fresh manure, a flatlander anxious
to be one of the guys, not asking too many
questions but knowing enough to step back
when one of the girls raised her rump.

Then one afternoon the cows were gone –
the stalls mucked out, gutters free of manure,
a snow machine up on blocks, the barn full of echoes.

His son and grandson chose logging
over milking. Better money, shorter hours,
though his grandson says he'd come back
in a heartbeat if he could make a living at it,
the lament of every dairyman up and down
this valley – costs eighteen bucks to produce
a hundred-weight that sells for eleven ninety-five.
"Show me how that works and I'll see tits on a mule!"
George once said, elbowing me in the ribs.

Now George boards heifers for a neighbor
who's still making a go of it. With the last
of the Ayrshires out to pasture, George slips
a wire loop over the gate post. His knees shot
after decades of squatting to wipe teats clean
and palm suction cups onto swelling udders,
it takes him long minutes to get out there,

but nothing keeps this old farmer
from the few chores he can still finish
despite needing two canes.

I see George now and again. We talk about the weather,
how someday he'll think about getting a pair of new knees.
I always look in each time I drive by. Today
George watches his heifers head out to pasture,
looks west to cumulus full of rain.
Propping one cane against the fence,
he hikes up his pants before going back inside.

6. Last Word

There's always more mystery.
Anais Nin

Another Day

She left the blue dress
hanging because it hadn't dried.
After last night's rain,
the wet cloth sags the line.
She stands at the kitchen window,
imaging the weight of water-
soaked cotton, the dampness
binding her hips, heavy
on her breasts. She wishes
she'd brought it in to finish drying
so she'd be wearing it when,
her head bent to washing beets,
dirt swirling down the drain,
he'd nuzzle her from behind,
slip the blue dress from her shoulders
where it would pool at her feet.

Acknowledgements

To Amelia, with love and light.
To Horace and Laurie, who gave me the springboard.
To Daniel Goodyear MD, with gratitude.

————————

My thanks and appreciation to the publications in which these poems first appeared.

"Claiming the Land," *Sow's Ear Poetry Review*
"The Plow Guy Makes Do," *Off the Coast*

I am grateful to these writers, mentors, places, family, and friends who have inspired me along the way and help keep me firing on all cylinders.

Emily Laurence Baker
David Baker
Robert Baker
Jeanne Marie Beaumont
Maryellen Bock
John Clarke
Pat Daneman
Bill Dart
Ian Frisch
Dwight and Joyce Fowler
John Gardner
Paul Hagar
Galen Green
Winslow Green
Bruce Hermann
Nancy Kerr
Fred Kerrick
Susanna Lang
My Champlain College students
Keith Oppenheim
J. Stephen Rhodes
Tim Seibles
Baron Wormser
Writers Colony at Dairy Hollow
Stonecoast Program/University of Southern Maine

My deepest thanks to my teacher and mentor, Lesléa Neuman for her astute, refined editor's eye and sound guidance on this collection.

Gratitude to Marc Estrin and Donna Bister of Fomite Press, who brought this book into the light.

About the Author

Photo: Sharon Coleman

Warren Baker hangs onto the tops of maple trees pitching in a stiff south wind, navigates the crags and valleys of black locust bark, and sits in the globe of a raindrop shuddering at the end of a pine needle. He loves Corgis, cats and gardening. Warren ran a poultry farm in Vermont and drove flatbeds laden with apples out of orchards in the rolling hills of south-central Pennsylvania. He worked in factories and warehouses. He sold woodstoves. He was a radio station copywriter and operations manager. As a community newspaper editor, Warren won awards from the Vermont Press Association for editorial writing. He earned an MFA from the Stonecoast Program at the University of Southern Maine. Warren retired as a professor and former director of the Professional Writing Program at Champlain College. He writes novels and plays. He lives with Sharon Coleman, his wife, in Burlington.

www.ingramcontent.com/pod-product-compliance
Lightning Source LLC
Chambersburg PA
CBHW031445120626
46545CB00006B/2553